Outstanding

MUSLIM PARENTS

MUSLIMS PARENTING ON PURPOSE: VOLUME 1

BUILDING THE FOUNDATION FOR OUR CHILDREN'S MUSLIM IDENTITY

NAZIR AL-MUJAAHID

(NADHEER BINNASEEB)

For information address Outstanding Muslim Parents Press Subsidiary Rights Department, 6650 West State Street, Suite 163 Wauwatosa, WI 53213

For information about special discounts for bulk purchases, please contact Outstanding Muslim Parents, Inc. at 866.812.7688 or business@outstandingmuslimparents.com

Designed by Faatimah Al-Mujaahid

Manufactured in the united states of America

Muslims Parenting on Purpose: Volume 1

Building The Foundation for our Children's Muslim Identity

Nazir Al-Mujaahid

ISBN: 978-0-9892051-0-8

Dedication

This book is dedicated to Allah t'ala for all the favors He has bestowed upon me and my family; in creating and bringing me to this world, His Love, His Mercy, His Graciousness, His Forgiveness, His Compassion, His Relentlessness, and His Bounty are above any person like me to be able to thank Him enough and to praise Him. To you O Allah, I am dedicating this book.

Ya Allah!   Accept my humble effort and help me to disseminate the information to those who need it.

Ya Allah!   Make this humble work worthy of You

Ya Allah!   Keep me on the straight path

Ya Allah!   Forgive my shortcomings

Ya Allah!   Help me to live as a Muslim and to die as a Mu'min

Ya Allah!   Let me be summoned on the Day of Judgment with the Prophets, Martyrs, and the Noble Believers.

Ameen

A Note to You, the Reader
Bismillah arRahmaan arRaheem

As salaamu 'alaykum wa rahmatullah,

As a trainer, coach, speaker, and full time father I have had the opportunity to work with remarkable individuals from all over the world, alHamdulillah. Many of the lessons in my book are syntheses of my experiences and interactions with my family, family of friends, and interactions with audiences and clients that I have worked with.

With the help of Allah, I've done my best in putting things together so that they are palatable and more importantly actionable so that you can benefit right away and keep the lessons with you over time.

Also, please know that I am a Muslim father that is concerned about the state of our Muslim youth, starting with my own. I am still raising my children and learning every day. My youngest is just over 6 months old at this time and we have much more knowledge with which to raise him with then we had 18 years ago ☺.

Please understand that I am NOT a medical doctor, licensed psychologist, psychotherapist, psychiatrist, neuroscientist, financial or legal strategist, or anything else that ends with "ist". I am a student and serve others with what I've learned in hopes to gain the pleasure of Allah t'ala. I am sharing what my family and I have learned from these fields and none of the information I share is intended, nor should it be construed, to be professional medical, psychological, financial, or legal advice. If you need assistance in those areas, consult area specific certified professionals. I am not responsible for anything bad or good that happens as a result of your doing what I advise in this book. Indeed, the whole premise of this book is empowering you with strategies that you believe are beneficial for your family.

May Allah make you successful in this life and the next and cause your children to be a blessing for you now and especially later, ameen!   Nazir Al-Mujaahid

May Allah protect and keep us and our children on the straight path and never have to inform us of a child not belonging to our family like He informed Prophet Noah (عليه الصلاة و السلام), *ameen.*

وَنَادَىٰ نُوحٌ رَّبَّهُ, فَقَالَ رَبِّ إِنَّ ٱبْنِي مِنْ أَهْلِي وَإِنَّ وَعْدَكَ ٱلْحَقُّ وَأَنتَ أَحْكَمُ ٱلْحَٰكِمِينَ ﴿٤٥﴾

قَالَ يَٰنُوحُ إِنَّهُۥ لَيْسَ مِنْ أَهْلِكَ ۖ إِنَّهُۥ عَمَلٌ غَيْرُ صَٰلِحٍ فَلَا تَسْـَٔلْنِ مَا لَيْسَ لَكَ بِهِۦ عِلْمٌ ۖ إِنِّيٓ أَعِظُكَ أَن تَكُونَ مِنَ ٱلْجَٰهِلِينَ ﴿٤٦﴾

And Noah called to his Lord and said, "My Lord, indeed my son is of my family; and indeed, Your promise is true; and You are the Most Just of Judges!" He said, "O Noah, indeed he is not of your family; indeed, he is [one whose] work was other than righteous, so ask Me not for that about which you have no knowledge. Indeed, I advise you, lest you be among the ignorant." *Qur'an Surah Hud 45-46*

In the name of Allah, The Most Gracious, The Most Merciful

FOREWORD

Muslims Parenting on Purpose! When I first heard the title
of this book, it immediately appealed to me both because of
the topic and because it was written by a father. It is a book I
wish had been available to me 40 years ago when I started
my family. I was definitely NOT parenting on purpose; I
was caught in an avalanche of biology struggling to come to
grips with my swiftly changing life circumstances. I was just
trying to keep my head above water and thoughtful
introspective parenting was playing a far second to survival.
I believe that if we are honest with ourselves, many of us
might admit a similar entrée into parenthood.

Tabarakallah, in this, his first book, Author Nazir Al-
Mujaahid aka Nadheer bin Naseeb builds on the Qur'an, the
Sunnah and his rich personal experience as an engaged,
conscious father to his 8 children to create a constructive
compilation of observations, insights, self-reflective
exercises and planning tools -- in short an enunciated
parenting approach for the consideration of the Muslim
reader. His straightforward style and timely references to the
world around us makes this an easy read not to be mistaken
for a no-brainer.

In shaa Allah, for those of us who are walking the
challenging path of parenting our children in the troubling
times in which we now live, Br. Nadheer's approach will
give us structure, support and encouragement to carry on.
For those of us who are anticipating parenthood or who are
currently parenting off-the-cuff, his reflections will help
create a road map with which to start (or restart) our journey.
If each of us takes the opportunity and methodology offered
within these pages to conduct an honest, in-depth

examination of our performance as parents and explore creative purposeful tactics for improvement, we should come away with a fresh perspective, some new ideas, and a deepened appreciation of the seriousness of our role as parents. Our children will thank us, if not now, later, in shaa Allah.

Intentional parenting -- parenting on purpose – should be like any other act of worship we perform as Muslims; we must bring our full conscious intention to the task if we desire the full reward for this awesome responsibility and opportunity. Surely, it is a trust from Allah for which we will be held accountable of that Day.

May Allah, subhana wa ta'ala, forgive our dear brother Nadheer and reward him for the best of his intentions and efforts both in his parenting and in his preparing this reminder for the Muslims. May his book be an ongoing sadaqa for him that benefits him and his family in this life and in the Hereafter.

Sabriyya Abdur-Rauf (Um Kathir)

◆————————————————————◆

Um Kathir is mother of 10 birth children and 2 step daughters, and the grandmother of 45 (May Allah bestow His blessings on them all.) She is owner and primary consultant of Y & S Institute, LLC., a professional and organizational development firm. She is a certified Doula, Nutritional Herbologist, and an aspiring midwife. She can be contacted at sabriyya@ysinstitute.org and birthphases.com

INTRODUCTION

Bismillah arRahmaan arRaheem

This book is a direct challenge to you as a Muslim who has a child or children or plan to sometime soon. I want to challenge you on the concept of ihsaan (excellence) and encourage you to practice ihsaan when it comes to parenting. This book isn't just to give you a few tips on how to deal with a few challenges and getting over a hump or two though you will certainly get those types of jewels inside. The book you hold in your hands is not meant to be a pleasure read that you say, "oh that's a good idea" or "I'll do that one exercise later".

In the pages ahead, you will find pragmatic, often counterintuitive guide that cuts through the clutter of bad advice and lays a solid foundation where there were many cracked and indeed no foundation at all! There will be exercises that are intended to get you into gear and cause you to workout your parenting skills frequently. If you don't use the parenting muscle you have, you may be directly contributing to the world of Muslims that are confused as their identity and weak in their worship to the Most High.

We must face the face that today we have an identity crisis. Our families are breaking up faster than ever and our children are leaving the fold of Islam, if not by declaration, then many by action. To not know how to deal with new situations that are arising that may not have affected us in such a way when we were growing up can be draining and demand more of our energy to figure out and this is where we provide outstanding solutions for today's problems.

We may not have had the privilege to meet yet, but I'm guessing that you have the same concerns as a parent that my family and I do. I'm also guessing that there are things you would like to do differently than your parents did while you were growing up. I'm convinced that the foundation and lessons you will soon learn are not just for you at this time in your life, but the framework can be applied to your children when they, if Allah wills, get married and make you a grandparent (if that hasn't already happened).

You will notice quickly that this isn't a lecturing type of book and that the structure may be a bit different than you are used to. However I'm confident that you will appreciate the style, stories, and exercises that have been poured into these pages for you to rise up to the next plane of possibilities as an outstanding parent!

To help people reach a higher plane, I've spent over 14 years now studying everything I could get my hands on in the fields of psychology, human achievement and potential, leadership, team work, high performance, neuroscience, and of course the lessons that Allah has provided us in the Quran with the lives of the Prophets and their unique dynamics. It is important that your change first be internal and you make a conscious decision to be open and critical of what you learn so that it can shape your parenting without losing who *you truly are.*

2

INTRODUCTION

I believe that it is due time that we parents are more strategic and purposeful in our parenting. Our children need us more than ever with so many things fighting for their attention especially with any electronic device handy. It may not matter in the long run how much time is put in as what is put into the time that matters. If we want more and we want better for our children in this crazy world that we live in, then we must do something different, do something better, and do something that others may consider crazy and I propose to say that is actually parenting on purpose because once we put our energies into parenting, then we fulfill one of the most important roles that Allah t'ala has blessed up with.

As society continues its mad rush towards more materialism and negating religious values while promoting immorality, it is our vision that they are directly attacking while the media continually works to recruit our children to their way of thinking. As parents that are not on the sideline watching the game of life go by, we must remember that we are in the game and that Allah t'ala has allowed us to be here at this moment for a reason so we must move forward and play the game while using the best plays we know how. This book can be considered a playbook of sorts as you can garner some specifics and guiding principles that will assist you in your decision making. The best playbooks don't only deal with offense, but they also know the importance of a strong defense and the pages ahead won't disappoint you in sha Allah.

As a father I share my perspective in great detail but just know that any introspection would be incomplete without the women that help me to be the best husband and father I can be. My mother provided great insight, many times on 'what not to do', though she is yet to become Muslim and I ask Allah to open her heart and guide her to this deen, ameen.

We have an abundant and glorious Islamic past and though our Ummah is currently going through a period of transition, we can change that when we remember that as long as we do all we can with what we have and empower our children to do more as our gifts to the future then we can honestly say that we have strived for ihsaan in our parenting which is none other than OUTSTANDING!

I pray that you finish the book AND complete the exercises while striving for ihsaan and that Allah t'ala makes the path to success easy for you and your loved ones, ameen.

Your family is ready, they are waiting, are you ready? If so, make a commitment to yourself to finish this book properly, turn the page, and let's get busy!

Chapter 1   Parenthood Begins

4am, mid-September 1995 – I was awakened by a loud
scream from my wife as she grasped her belly. This wasn't a
Braxton-Hicks contraction. This was something much harder
and more real -- something she had never felt before and
something that would be the beginning of changing our lives
forever. It was true labor! Official parenthood was racing
toward us and my anxiety meter was competing for first
place. But I tried my best to remain the supportive and
accommodating husband to my wife who was suffering much
more than me.

We both had genetic titles: I was a son first, then a brother,
and then a husband and she was a daughter, sister, and then a
wife but neither of us had yet been promoted to parent and
now we were fast approaching that title with little knowledge
but plenty of love.

Of course we'd already shopped and had clothes, diapers,
toys, bibs, crib, car seat, swing, and all of the things babies
usually have to make things comfortable. We had the
authentic Islamic rituals down packed and knew to call the
adhan in her ear, have a righteous person make du'a for her
and let her taste a softened date, and prepare to name her. We
had her name picked out and knew what she would be
wearing when we left the hospital, in shaa Allah. We were as
prepared as we could be with no experience and only our
mother's experience of labor with our younger siblings to
look back on for guidance.

Alhamdulillah, 18 hours after the labor began, our daughter
was born healthy, happy, and a blessed addition to our family
that now totaled 3 people! As a father, the experience was
like no other and the gratefulness to Allah in His infinite

wisdom was manifest. Now that the title of father, dad, and Abu was upon me and I felt like I had new powers. I had to protect this little one, provide for her, to make sure she was well educated, and to do my best to make sure she was grounded in Islam. This new title of parent proved to bring with it some of the most difficult tasks I had ever known. Allah provided the abundance of love we would pour into our new daughter and as new parents we emerged more selfless and with expanded vision, thinking, and hopes alongside our increasing fears of the unknown.

We were overwhelmed with questions. *"What will happen if we don't do a good job raising her? What if people try to hurt her? Growing up in a non-Muslim society there is so much negative pressure, what can we do? What about the Muslim schools and how they operate? What about her future friends and peer pressure? What if she deals with things we had to deal with when we were young and growing up? Who else will protect her if something happens to us? What family can we count on to be there when they are all non-Muslims? Who after us, her parents, will have her best interests in mind? What resources do we have to raise her up on Islam? What guides are there that incorporate how to live Islamically in the West and keep a strong Muslim identity?*

Yes, we asked ourselves each of these and many other questions and often the answers were not to our liking because we understood that the deck is stacked heavily against us living in the West and is not much better in other areas as well.

PARENTHOOD BEGINS

Chapter 2 Preparation for being a parent

بسم الله الرحمن الرحي

هُنَالِكَ دَعَا زَكَرِيَّا رَبَّهُ، قَالَ رَبِّ هَبْ لِى مِن لَّدُنكَ ذُرِّيَّةً طَيِّبَةً
إِنَّكَ سَمِيعُ الدُّعَاءِ ﴿٣٨﴾

*"My Lord! Grant me from [your mercy] pure offspring.
Indeed, you are listener of invocations."
(Surah Ale-Imran 3:38)*

Now that I'm officially a parent, what next?

I've helped raise my younger siblings and changed other
babies' diapers and have gathered experience from those
things, but those babies weren't my flesh and blood. I've read
some books on parenting and some of them have opposing
views and most seem to give good advice while others take
an overly analytical approach reminiscent of programming
one's child like a supercomputer.

Analyzing my research and experiences, I quickly realized
that many of us as parents – or soon to be parents -- have the
same concerns. We want our children to be healthy,
intelligent, prepared for the real world and for them to have it
better than we did. As Muslims living in the West, our
particular circumstances may differ from our non-Muslim
counterparts and even from Muslims living in Islamic
countries; however, our basic desires remain relatively the
same. Those of us who are attempting to actively prepare
ourselves go to great lengths to uncover insights into the
"how" of achieving a better life for our offspring.

In order to make sure we were well equipped for our lifelong parenting journey, my wife and I visited Islamic libraries and bookstores searching for some type of guide for raising strong Muslim children in the West. Unfortunately, we were deeply disappointed because of the scarcity of books and audios containing basic advice relative to our situation. This was the first time I realized that one of the biggest challenges Muslim parents have is the lack of access to quality resources that address our parenting needs and concerns as Muslims.

I am a firm believer in learning lessons from others' mistakes. When we learn from others, we save time and stress because we don't have to figure everything out for ourselves. Imagine if we had to learn all about coding for computers and fiber optic cables in order to use the internet! Let's be honest, we all like shortcuts and if there were some shortcuts on how to raise children, we'd likely be all ears and ready to learn more. Unfortunately, there are no shortcuts; our children aren't computers so we can't just install some software program and out pops what we desire in good behavior and learning! If only it were that easy!

Gratefully, there are a set of rules that govern our behavior as parents and those rules are often as timeless as they are enlightening and these rules are called…

PREPARATION FOR BEING A PARENT

Chapter 3   Principles

We know that our children are an amanah (a trust) from Allah. They are in our care for a short time and we must use what tools we have to assist and care for them as part of Allah's creation. There are principles that guide our behavior and our life collectively as Muslims and there are principles that specifically affect our relationships with others at home, with relatives, in the masjid, in the workplace, and in our larger public spheres. Our parenting principles go a long way toward determining what type of atmosphere we provide for our children and likewise greatly influence how much sanity we have left at the end of the day.

What is problematic is that many of us are unaware of what our principles are. We muddle through each day shifting from one set of behaviors to the other frustrated or clueless about why our relationship with our children and their relationships with each other are teetering on the edge of total unpredictability and utter chaos. The saving grace is that once we are aware of our principles, we now have a critical guide we can use to navigate our course. Just as most of us when traveling someplace we have never visited, will use a map on how to get there -- whether it be a physical map, GPS system, or turn-by-turn directions. Principles may not necessarily be turn-by-turn directions but they can help define the overall terrain, upcoming boundaries and barriers, and our general heading.

My goal, here is to offer what I have learned about adopting conscious principles and "Parenting on Purpose" -- and that is a good place to start!

Parenting on Purpose -- In today's fast paced society with messages bombarding us via our 'smart devices', televisions, cars, and anywhere and everywhere in our public and private spaces, we must be vigilant in our quest to raise righteous Muslim children. The *Trial and Error* method of parenting usually ends up very disappointing. This method will leave most of us feeling as if we are on *trial* and we have executed many *errors*!

I'd like to share with you the experience of one of my dear friends whom I will refer to hear as Ali (all names have been changed). He was one of the first Muslims I met after I accepted Islam. He and his wife had a young one year old son at the time and I recall how loving their family was and how happy my friend was to be following this wonderful deen of Islam. He shared with me how he named his child after a great prophet who was the son of a prophet and father of a prophet. He shared with me how he had aspirations of his son learning the Quran from a young age and leading future generations on the clear path of Islam. We both studied together and visited each other often and about a year later, I became a father. Then, we had one more thing in common -- we both had young children, ma shaa Allah. I shared with him the things I wanted to teach my daughter and how I planned to have so many things set up for her and he shared more of what he wanted for his son.

As our children grew older and we both expanded our families with more children there were a few times that I remember distinctly when I offered advice to my friend and mentor because I saw seeds being sown that could hurt later. I recall celebrating 'Eid ul adha and 'Eid ul fitr with my entire family and the Muslim community. I saw Ali's entire family and searched for him, but he wasn't there -- he was at work. He was able to make his own schedule because he ran the facility where he worked, so I was really concerned that he had chosen not to attend the 'Eid. When I got the chance, I informed him that I felt he needed to be present as an example for his children and support for his wife because we as Muslim parents should make our holiday celebrations exceptional in our children's eyes (especially when the non-Muslims holidays are promoted so heavily and many Muslim families are losing their children to these non-Muslim musings). He heard me but didn't heed what I said and as the years passed, he continued to miss Islamic events that his family attended including salatul jumu'ah at the masjid. These choices began to take their toll on his family.

As his little boy grew older (into what was not a young *'man'*), I noticed a change in him when I asked him how his father was doing. His response was the somber, "He's good, alhamdulillah," with a look of *'I wish he was here to tell you how he was.'* He was the only other male besides his father in the family as he was the oldest of many sisters. His language, dress, and demeanor were becoming more and more concerning. I knew the pull and attraction of kufr because that was where I used to dwell; I am very grateful that Allah blessed me with Islam and removed me from jahiliyyah. Interestingly, people who lived in kufr and ran away from it to Islam tend to be able to see clearly when Muslims are running from Islam to kufr; even their parents may not be able to see it.

As time passed and his son reached puberty and was evolving into a strong man, his transformation was almost total. His personality began to take on that street swag and his clothes reflected the same. He lost the adab he used to have naturally and his eyes wandered to staring when he should have been lowering his gaze. It wasn't long before hearing that he got into some quarrel with someone over a girl and that he completely abandoned Islam and told his parents that he no longer believed in Allah. That was a sad day indeed and caused his parents to cry many tears. The pain of regret set in with his father, my dear friend.

It became clear that all of the advice and warnings he had received began making sense to him. His regret for his negligence of his responsibilities and his carelessness of the trust that Allah had granted him and his wife turned his parenting practices around. Thankfully, Ali and his wife decided to focus on their younger children in order to protect them from harm and from following the example of their older brother.

There are numerous lessons that we can learn from this situation. I encourage you to learn the lessons from good and not-so-good situations because you have been made aware of them for a reason. In my case, watching this painful situation unfold in the life of my friend was one of the inspirations for developing a conscious approach to parenting my own children and later the desire to share what I had learned in the Outstanding Muslim Parents Academy.
(For more information, visit
OutstandingMuslimParents.com/OMPAcademy)

The upcoming lesson that I would like to share is what I have come to call the **Three Basic Parenting Roles** or the **Three C's** and these are roles that all parents have by default. We'll discuss each of these roles in detail as we progress throughout the book. In shaa Allah, once we understand the significance of each role and begin to integrate them into our daily lives as parents, we can begin to see above average results in our journey.

PRINCIPLES

Chapter 4   The First Parental Role

The Celebrity – C 1

Celebrities are well known people, nothing more, nothing less. People tend to know them and follow them for better or for worse. Many times we hear of celebrities involved in scandals or atrocious behavior and other times we hear of celebrities involved in charity work, sports, or cause-based missions. Like it or not, there are little ones that think the entire world of us and no matter what we think of the term, we as parents must recognize that we *are* celebrities to our little ones.

In most cases, when our children are very young, we are all they know and who they see on a constant basis. When they are in trouble or in need, they are not able to call up friends or other people for comfort besides perhaps a sibling, our little ones' mini-celebrities. Mothers usually benefit the most from and suffer the most from being the Superstar! Mom is definitely the best friend, the one that can calm the child when upset, and the one that the child wants to be with over anyone else. It is a mercy that Allah provides comfort, love, and support in the arms of our mothers no matter how old we get, alhamdulillah.

Taking ownership of the CELEBRITY role is definitely easier said than done. A celebrity has many functions and responsibilities. As a celebrity, we are that role model, we are the ones that our little ones look up to both literally and figuratively, and we are the ones that our children believe and trust to protect them. When our children see us praying, they imitate us. When our children ask us questions and we answer, they believe us. When our children come to us for

16

advice, it is because they recognize that their information is limited but Mom or Dad may know the answer or may be able to help. The most important thing we can do as a celebrity is to be consistent and congruent with our children.

Practicing what we preach is relieving and reassuring for a child; on the contrary saying or sending the message 'do what I say do, don't do as I do' can erode trust for a lifetime. I vividly recall watching my father taking a cigarette and lighting it up when I was 5 years old. He noticed me watching and told me to not smoke cigarettes because they were bad for me. I was immediately confused because I wondered to myself, "If they're bad for me, aren't they bad for you too?" Then when he wasn't looking, I promptly went over to the ash tray picked up a cigarette butt, lit it, and took a puff and after choking I decided that it wasn't for me!

Many people believe that children are extremely resilient, so they trivialize children's emotional crises. When we look at the emotional makeup of a child, all we have to do is go back to when we were younger and see how things *felt* to us. We felt when something was wrong. We perceived things as enormously impactful to our lives and happiness. But now, when we look back on our feelings and perceptions, we might be amused or see things more clearly. We were all bundles of emotion and had a long way to go. There are, however, some experiences that can scar children deeply over the long haul.

There is one emotion that I can remember more vividly than most others -- the stinging pain of betrayal I felt when I learned that my parents worked so hard to lie to me. This story goes back to my life before Islam. While it is a story about Christmas, and no longer applies to my way of life, I purposefully use it here as it is becoming more and more common to see Muslim children celebrating Christian holidays such as Christmas and others without any clear understanding.

Growing up as a Christian, I remember being 5 years old and my father waking me up very early on Christmas morning (December 25th) and he picked me up and took me out on our 2nd floor porch in the snow and told me to look in the sky because Santa Claus had just left! After I looked and looked and was unable to see anything, he brought me back into the house where I saw all sorts of gifts under the Christmas tree including a race track (obviously for me) and other gifts that were wrapped up with my name on them. I felt so good, happy, and thankful that Santa Claus brought me these gifts.

Well, as you know Santa didn't bring anything (and you should also know that if you unscramble the word Santa indeed spells Satan). My parents eventually caved in and confirmed that Santa wasn't real after some child I didn't know told me the unvarnished truth. I recall my heart dropping as they informed me that there were more characters that weren't real like the Easter Bunny and the Tooth Fairy. I could never understand why my parents perpetuated these myths that ended up hurting me so badly, but I do recall experiencing a type of hurt that I never felt before -- the hurt of betrayal. My parents to whom I looked for absolute guidance and protection were lying to me while telling me not to lie. They told me to do what they said but not as they did, and all I could think was I didn't like that hurting feeling. This is an example of what **NOT TO DO**! Don't abuse your celebrity status with betrayal unless you want to regret it later.

Alhamdulillah, we have been blessed with a more positive methodology. We have the best example in the Prophet Muhammad (عليه الصلاة و السلام) and we know to follow his Sunnah because he was the best of mankind. When we want to know of the best character, we look to our Prophet (السلام

و الصلاة عليه) whether that means his example as a father,
husband, statesman, fighter, teacher, neighbor or friend. Our
children look to our behavior to see what is correct. There are
two sayings I'm reminded of: "Your actions are speaking so
loudly I can hardly hear what you are saying" and "Actions
speak louder than words." Said more eloquently in the
Qur'an and emphasizing the strong aversion we should have
to this practice, Allah instructs us:

$$ يَـٰٓأَيُّهَا ٱلَّذِينَ ءَامَنُوا۟ لِمَ تَقُولُونَ مَا لَا تَفْعَلُونَ ﴿٢﴾ $$

$$ كَبُرَ مَقْتًا عِندَ ٱللَّهِ أَن تَقُولُوا۟ مَا لَا تَفْعَلُونَ ﴿٣﴾ $$

*"Oh, you who believe! Why do you say that which you do not do? Most
hateful it is with Allah, that you say what you do not do."*
(Qur'an 61: 2-3)

It is with this reminder that we should view the potentially
demoralizing effect upon our children (and upon their
perceptions of us as parents) that may come when they begin
to analyze whether what we did when they were young and
as they grew actually matched what we said and what we
currently say.

As we go on to further explore the definition of the Celebrity,
we see that Celebrities are trend setters. They tend to
influence people in many industries, the fashion industry a
most easily recognizable one where so and so is wearing
shoes by Designer X or sporting a new handbag or look from
Designer Y's new line of suits. There are 'Best Dressed' and
'Worst Dressed' lists yearly and even quarterly on
supermarket shelves and gossip magazines.

Considering the Power of Societal Influence

While speaking on the topic of hijab and the khimar specifically, I want to remind you that we are bombarded daily with images on what beauty is supposed to be whether it's on a commercial or cartoon. We need to be cognizant of the programming that our children are receiving from the many different forms of media that they are exposed to.

In the 1930's and 1940's there were famous doll experiments done with African American children in segregated schools which showed the inherent self-hatred that African American children had developed. When all of the children preferred to play

Well how do you think this relates to our children as they grow from toddlers to adolescents? When they are young, it doesn't matter what they wear because they don't have a sense of fashion or flair for the decorative in clothing, so it's so easy to take the opportunity to dress up our little ones in cute *(gaudy!)* clothing that gets attention, smiles, and sometimes even laughs. As our children get older our sons and daughters tend to look at Mom and Dad's dress as what is acceptable.

They may imitate us when they are really young but as they grow older; they pick out their own clothes and likely have already decided what is socially acceptable because of what their parents wear.

This is an issue that is equally important for both boys and girls however the principles contained within the Islamic dress code differ when it comes to who is more distinguishable by their clothes as a Muslim.

For example, our boys and men

can and many times do blend in with the rest of Western society by not making any distinction in the clothing they choose to wear while still being compliant with hijab for males where our girls and women don't have the same option.

It never ceases to amaze me how our community has so many problems with our young girls not wanting to cover themselves properly when in public. We live in a society that tells us that the more a woman shows off her body (also known as her assets) the more she is free and freedom trumps everything else. When they aren't able to see our women's assets they figure the woman is oppressed simply because they are not able to enjoy the beauty Allah created for a special person. Odd, indeed!

Let's also remember that the West proudly flaunts its designers who often are openly homosexual. The fact that men who don't like women but are an authority on what is beautiful in women has always puzzled me. We must be cognizant of such trickery and stand up for our deen and our daughters if we want to raise Muslim children with strength of character and love for Islam.

As the celebrity, we set the trends and since we already have a Sunnah and way of life to follow, it isn't that difficult to set a trend that is on the path of the truth. The challenge is that we must be doing it intentionally and avoid being haphazard in it. Don't wait to show interest in your daughter's appearance when your daughter is bra-shopping and taking pride in showing off her hair and curves. It is so much more challenging when we are forced into being reactive because we let the window of opportunity almost close shut before we take notice. Waiting until your daughter becomes of age may result in a challenging road ahead with your celebrity status diminishing along the way.

So this is where mom must do her part: dress according to what Islam dictates and do it in Celebrity fashion, that is, with confidence and minus any apologies. I'm not going to get into the fiqh of dress here because it is (or hopefully is) well known[1] already. However, I would like to share an example here from my personal experience. My wife and I came across some great information when my oldest was just a teeny weeny toddler. A brother was talking about how to help your daughters love the headscarf (khimar) and he was encouraging us to compliment and praise them when they wore the khimar at a young age. When our children were young they would get into everything including mom's khimars. I never had to demand my daughters wear their khimars; they did it on their own imitating their mom and started at about 5 years old. Interestingly, some people thought we 'forced' our children to wear it at such a young age and they were surprised to find that our daughters wanted to wear it on their own. My wife was approached and reminded many times that it isn't fard (waajib/obligatory) on our young adolescent girls and that she shouldn't be so strict on them. My wife graciously reminded the other sisters that our daughters found joy in imitating her and that she was grateful for that. She also reminded them that we live in the West and must adhere to our deen in public and in private because too many of us are losing our deen and we didn't want that for our family.

So when *your* daughter takes and puts a khimar on her head like she sees her mother do daily when she prays, then praise her, call others to see her and have them lavishly lay it on. This reinforces the belief that modesty and covering are beautiful and it makes her feel good. What you are doing is using your celebrity status to water and provide sunshine to

---

[1] Quran, Surah Nur 24: 30-31

that growing seed and in shaa Allah you will recognize significant confidence growing in that baby girl.

As fathers, we must realize how important it is that we reinforce what beauty is to our daughters and sons. Our media bombards us with sexy women and sexy men, constantly telling us what is beautiful, alluring, desirable, and a symbol of love, all for the purpose of selling a product or service. As they are selling us these products and services, they are selling us the culture more than anything and we must be vigilant so that we don't fall into a trap that we may not be able to extricate ourselves from. So it is our responsibility to remind our daughters and our spouses of how beautiful they are not only due to the physical beauty with which Allah created them but even more so due to their submission to Allah in Islam. As fathers, we have a very important role in our home as celebrities because we are seen as the symbol of strength and leadership. After all, we are the providers (for the most part) and we are the ones that the family looks to for protection against outside forces and we are honored with the title of Imam.

Further, it is just as important for the father to pay attention to what he *does* as it is important for him to pay attention to what he *does not do*. When we recognize that our children in their limited understanding are making assumptions, analysis, and decisions based on incomplete yet true-to-them information, it is critical that we are seen in the best light. If we want to aid our children to be on their deen, we must be on ours. Simple logic, right? Unfortunately, if you are a father who works outside your home for hours a day and are exhausted when you get home and simply want some quiet or relaxation in front of the television or computer, then be aware of how that appears to your child.

Sadly, the reality is that the United States Department of Education did a study which indicated that US mothers spend less than 30 minutes a day talking with their children and fathers spend even less. There have been other study findings that show that many fathers spend less than 30 minutes a week speaking with their children. One-to-one conversation averaged 9 ½ minutes for at-home mothers and 10.7 minutes for working mothers, and far less for fathers., The stunning thing is that in his ***Read Aloud Handbook***, internationally acclaimed educator and author Jim Trelease[2] pointed out that the average adult parent in the US spends 6 hours per week shopping and 30 hours per week watching television, in contrast to daily time spent with school-aged offspring.

Most parents find the time to put in a full workday, take a full complement of coffee breaks, eat lunch and dinner, read the newspaper, watch the nightly newscast or ball game, do the dishes, talk on the phone for 30 minutes ... drive to the mall, and never miss that favorite prime-time show.[3]

With this information, we should have a clearer insight as to our own celebrity status in the eyes of our children – are we a celebrity that shuns the very ones that Allah has given us as a trust or are we appreciating them and intentionally caring for them in a manner that is real and meaningful to them? Own your celebrity status and know that your biggest fans are the ones that carry your DNA!

---

[2] Jim Trelease is a well-known US educator and author who was a pivotal force between 1979 and 2008 for the read-aloud movements in the United States and abroad.

[3] Calkins, Lucy, Raising Lifelong Learners: A Parents' Guide, Da Capo Press, 1998

Your C 1 Self-Assessment

So now it's time for your first of several official homework assignments. (Yes you are a parent, but you still have homework!) I'm requesting that you do some self-reflection and assess your personal Celebrity or C1 status. Find a quiet moment to answer the following questions in a personal journal or, if you prefer, on the C 1 online document at *OutstandingMuslimParents.com/c1* Your thoughtful answers should help you become a more effective Celebrity.

1. **Name a situation where you remember your Celebrity role in action,** *no matter your child's age.*

2. **List a time when you could have utilized your status better?**

3. **How can I take better advantage of my Celebrity status with my children overall?**

4. **What opportunities can I take with my children on a daily/weekly basis?**

5. **What engaging conversations can I have with my children that teach a lesson?**

6. **Considering the ages of your children, how can your role as the Celebrity be more effective?**

REMEMBER – You can print your C 1 worksheet at:

OutstandingMuslimParents.com/c1

Chapter 5   The Second Parental Role

The Confidant – C 2

A Confidant is one to whom secrets or private matters are disclosed. We as parents are the first and most important confidants that our children have. Many parents of older children wish their child would come and speak with them when they have personal issues or challenges that bother them instead of going to others that may or may not have their best interests in mind. Have we set the groundwork for this role? Of the three roles we are discussing in this book, this one requires us to be very intentional and requires us to continually grow in different areas of our lives.

As parents, we have experienced far more in our lives than our children; we have learned so much that enables us to decipher what is essential and what isn't; we have even forgotten so much that it would probably astound us. Many us of have forgotten more than our children currently know about life. Our voices and perspective are important to our children despite the fact that they may act otherwise, and it is crucial that we keep our voices relevant.

As a Confidant, we seemingly have secret knowledge only because our children may lack the maturity to understand at an early age. It is comical (and sometimes bittersweet) to reflect that like their parents, when our children get older and Allah expands their understanding, they will begin to recognize some of the lessons we as parents taught them at an earlier stage in their lives. I am still learning lessons from my father, may Allah have mercy on him, and my mother, may Allah guide her to His deen, even though some of the lessons are decades old. It is not uncommon for me to hear

28

friends say, "*That* is what my grandfather meant when he told me that!" Alhamdulillah, the old adage that says, "When the student is ready, the teacher will appear," can also be rephrased as "When the child is ready, the lessons will sink in."

We, as Muslims, have an advantage over most parents on the planet in that we have a lifestyle that has already answered the most significant questions and provided us a way to live fully. We have Islam and we have the final Prophet and Messenger Muhammad bin Abdullah (عليه الصلاة و السلام) as the best example for mankind. So when it comes to questions about creation, our purpose on earth, how to behave in our daily lives, death, and the afterlife, we have the answer. What a relief! The challenge comes when we don't know how Islam applies to our daily lives and we aren't attempting to learn. This is neglectful and it usually happens when a parent feels that they are 'too busy' or will get to it later. In fact, it is procrastination!

Since Islam provides a complete way of life, we must be in tuned to today's society and its messages in order to be aware of the methods that Shaytan uses to influence our children in a subtle but deadly fashion. To further make my point, let's explore some prevalent social issues that may present an opportunity to explore your role as a Confidant to make my point.

Racism -- Today there is a lot of tribalism, nationalism, and racism within the ummah and we hate to admit it. I have experienced it first hand and have seen it even in the holy city of Makah while I was on hajj. Darker skinned people tend to get treated in an ill fashion in general in the West as a whole and throughout the world. We see its impact even more so when we consider the skin lightening creams that are so prevalent throughout the Muslim world in just about any pharmacy or grocery store. We have internalized this racism and it manifests itself in self-hatred, thus the desire to change one's skin color.

When our children must confront and tackle the important and ever so visible challenge of racism, tribalism, or nationalism, having the truth makes it much easier for us to teach our children the correct perspective. When our child wants to sort out why his classmate or even his teacher treats her in a racist manner, we can equip and comfort them by referring to the Quran, where Allah says:

يَـٰٓأَيُّهَا ٱلنَّاسُ إِنَّا خَلَقْنَـٰكُم مِّن ذَكَرٍ وَأُنثَىٰ وَجَعَلْنَـٰكُمْ شُعُوبًا وَقَبَآئِلَ لِتَعَارَفُوٓا۟ إِنَّ أَكْرَمَكُمْ عِندَ ٱللَّهِ أَتْقَىٰكُمْ إِنَّ ٱللَّهَ عَلِيمٌ خَبِيرٌ ﴿١٣﴾

"O mankind, indeed We have created you from male
and female and made you peoples and tribes that you
may know one another. Indeed, the most noble of you
in the sight of Allah is the most righteous of you.
Indeed, Allah is Knowing and Acquainted."
(Quran 49:13)

Furthermore, we can discuss with our children numerous authentic ahadith such as during the farewell khutbah of the Prophet Muhammad (عليه الصلاة و السلام) where he stated:

"All mankind is from Adam and Eve, an Arab
has no superiority over a non-Arab nor a non-
Arab has any superiority over an Arab; also a
white has no superiority over black nor does a

30

black have any superiority over white except
by piety and good action. Learn that every
Muslim is a brother to every Muslim and that
the Muslims constitute one brotherhood.
Nothing shall be legitimate to a Muslim which
belongs to a fellow Muslim unless it was given
freely and willingly. Do not, therefore, do
injustice to yourselves."

Sexuality -- Now let's talk about a second pervasive issue --
sex. I live in a different world than when my parents were
growing up. Back then in the era of black and white
television, you would not see couples in bed together. There
was a famous show called ***I Love Lucy*** where a woman name
Lucy and her husband Ricky Ricardo were married and on
this show they NEVER appeared in bed together! They
actually had separate beds because it was immoral and
considered taboo in society to show such a thing ... at that
time. WOW, how things have changed! Today you can turn
on the TV and see not only traditional married couples on
regular television in the bed, but you can see homosexual
couples that have adopted children in bed or kissing and so
on. The times have changed only in openness of these issues
because we know that this type of behavior isn't new. We
know of the destruction sent upon the people that Prophet Lut
(Lot) was sent to for their persistence in disobeying Allah.
The difference today is that homosexual behavior which
Islam forbids is now considered an issue like 'civil rights'.

As Confidants, we must know how to clearly and age
appropriately address such issues with our children and help
them put the diverse narratives in the proper perspective.

31

Here's how I addressed homosexuality. I showed my children some cartoon clips from when I was younger of Bugs Bunny, a well-known and beloved child's cartoon character of Warner Brother's studios. I showed them how he would frequently cross-dress, wearing women's clothing and make up, in order to disguise himself so he wouldn't be recognized by Elmer Fudd who was a human that hunted rabbits. Bugs Bunny went to such an extent that he even seduced Elmer Fudd and played up to him in a sexual fashion.

Now we as parents must ask ourselves, "What message is being sent to our children?" What were the creators of the show attempting to get across? What did our children see and how did they feel? Many times they (and we) might just laugh because it is supposed to be funny. However, this is an opportunity for us to educate our children. Ask them, "Do you think that Shaytan will come to you in a scary or an attractive way that looks like fun? We could share with them the hadith which describes Allah's creation of the Hellfire.

He *said to Jibreel,*

> *"Go to Hell and look at it and the punishments that I have prepared for its inhabitants.' Jibreel looked at Hell and found it extremely horrible, so he said to Allah, 'I swear by Your Grandeur that not a single person will hear of it except that he will avoid entering it.' Then Allah ordered Hell to be surrounded by desires and luxuries and said to Jibreel, 'Go back to it.' Jibreel returned to Hell and then said, 'I swear by Your Grandeur that no one will be able to escape from it.* Abu Daud

In my case, after showing my children these cartoons, I asked them about Prophet Lut, the nephew of our father Ibraheem (upon them be peace), and they informed me of the story of the People of Lut. Ma shaa Allah, with little prompting from me my older children were able to explain how this cartoon related to today's strong push for the homosexual agenda and they were able to draw the link to the devices Shaytan uses to lead us astray.

Holidays -- One last example of ways in which you use and can capitalize on your Confidant role is when dealing with the concept of celebrating holidays other than Eid ul Fitr or Eid ul Adha. Here in the West, the non-Muslims' holidays are an excellent opportunity to educate my children. It is amazing that when your children know the roots of how things originated, they feel so empowered and often take it upon themselves to share that newfound knowledge. Keep in mind; this increases your status on the Confidant meter as well. Take a holiday like Valentine's Day and its origins.

Many Muslim children are swayed to participate in one way or another even if they attend Muslim schools. However, when you do your research on who Mr. Valentine was, what his belief system was, and what he did, then you are empowered and can equip your children with the truth while opening their eyes and allowing them to see how people just blindly follow the traditions from the days of old without thinking. Doesn't this sound like how the Quraysh followed the religion of their fathers even though their fathers were in error?

Socio-Economic & Politics -- It doesn't matter if you apply this 'research and expose' program to holidays, vaccination programs, or sexual deviations. What matters is that you get your children's attention and teach them to see things clearly while gazing through an Islamic lens. This is especially easy nowadays with so much information at our fingertips.

When looking at the political climate throughout the world, it is not difficult to find a crisis affecting the Western world like the economic crisis that is crushing billions of people worldwide and wiping out the middle class in the US. Nor is it difficult to find a crisis in the Muslim world where drones are indiscriminately killing men, women, and children or governments are oppressing people by not ruling according to the method of our Prophet Muhammad (عليه الصلاة و السلام) and the four righteous khulafah.

Discuss these current events with your children, help them read between the lines of the traditional media outlets and guide them in questioning what they see, hear, or come across. Help them find reliable resources and relate what they uncover to the spiritual battle waged by Shaytan, whom Allah ta'ala has declared an open enemy to us. By beginning with educating and sensitizing our families to the affairs of the ummah, then expanding to our local communities with an eye and desire to impact our entire ummah, we can begin to counteract the division that is running rampant through the best Ummah that has ever been placed on this planet. We are commanded to be unified and surely those that are not concerned about the affairs of the ummah are not from it.[4]

In summary, the main thing we must keep in mind is that as a Confidant we must come from an Islamic perspective, including how we behave or conduct ourselves, in other words our adab, our Islamic character. We help our children explore how to behave in public and private, how to dress properly and the reasons why – always relating back to our core beliefs and practices as Muslims. These conversations

---

[4] Muslim

open the door for our children to share difficulties the encounter. They deepen our connection with our children and let them know that we welcome this time with them and will try our utmost to be a rich, reliable resource to them and a bridge to knowledge greater than our own. The benefit to us as parents is that we are forced to deepen and solidify our own understanding of so many life issues while we are serving in this significant role – the Confidant!

Your C 2 Self-Assessment

Now it time for your second homework assignment! In order to become more effective with your C 2 parental role, answer the following questions in a personal journal or using the document online by following this link. (*OutstandingMuslimParents.com/c2*)

1. **What issues of the day need to be addressed so that my child isn't easily swayed by Shaytan?**

2. **How am I currently infusing Islamic lessons into daily life so that my child sees Islam as relevant?**

3. **What do I need to learn more about in order to equip my children?**

4. **How have I already equipped my child as a Confidant?**

5. **What can I study so that I understand Islam better and am more prepared to equip my children?**

Access your C 2 worksheet at:

OutstandingMuslimParents.com/c2

Chapter 6   The Third Parental Role

The Coach – C 3

We all have seen coaches in action and perhaps have been affected by a coach at some time in our lives. People that are peak performers and operate at higher levels in the sports arena have coaches. We see an international array of coaches and coaching styles at the Olympics every four years. We see professional coaches get paid in the millions of dollars for leading their teams to victory or simply leading their teams.

There are numerous styles of coaching and many rewards and pitfalls that can affect coaches of all types. As parents, we are the first coach and usually the only lifelong coach our children have. We traditionally recognize our coaching when we are consciously trying to teach our child something and they may not understand or get it, something like potty training for example. We also see ourselves being the cheerleaders for our little ones when they are learning to walk or talk.

The secret that the best coaches have in common is they are able to see their player's strengths and weaknesses and find a way to help the player bring the best out in himself. A coach isn't there to complete the task or training for the player, but instead to get the player to bring their best and work hard to excel even his own perceptions of himself. As parents, we do the encouraging, cheerleading, celebrating, and especially the disciplining.

Let me be clear, discipline is NOT synonymous with punishment. The discipline I'm speaking of is adhering to the rules and principles as they apply in a situation. For example,

Islam is a religion of discipline and that is pretty easy to see, especially for non-Muslims. Muslims fast during Ramadan which isn't necessarily easy especially during the summer time. Muslims pray five times per day, and they must perform a physically and mentally challenging pilgrimage to the Ka'ba in Makkah at least once in their lifetimes if physically and financially possible.

The key to successful discipline is finding the emotional balance with your child. All of my children are different from one another. One is a genius artist who can compete with those three times her age especially since she has been creating art since she was about 6 years old and has finally hit double digits in age. Another is a Fashionista who coordinates clothing and styles like no other that I've seen. Yet another is a dinosaur and animal expert. (Maa shaa Allah, may Allah bless and protect them all.) Each of my children has different likes and dislikes which we all know to be natural; similarly, each of them has a different emotional level as well. To one you can joke about her smile while you better not do that with her sister without her taking it personally and feeling hurt. A great coach understands the needs of his team and helps bring out their strengths and pushes them to go further than they think possible. Discipline is one of the most misunderstood parts of parenting and if we understand it properly within the context of Islam, we can make sure we are leading a winning team known better as family. Our job as coaches can be a daunting task because coaches must have a plan and know how to execute the plan. When the Trial-and-Error (T&E) method of parenting is used, there is no plan. Not to fear, if you are in the T&E mode, we are going to take a look at how we can move forward to a more productive approach.

In order to craft a plan, we need first to have a desired result. We must first decide what we want to see our children winning at. This can be a challenge so I want you to answer these questions and really think them out. Do this for each one of your children.

What five things do I want my children to do when it comes to Islam? (i.e. praying, fasting, learning Quran, etc.)

1. _____

2. _____

3. _____

4. _____

5. _____

What is the first step required in order to have my children _(Insert one of the five here)_ **when it comes to Islam?** (Do this for each of the five areas)

What resources do I already have at my disposal or what resources can I acquire easily that can assist in achieving

_____? (books, articles, websites, masjid classes, etc…)

How much time will this require? (daily/weekly/monthly)

What will I establish as an accountability measure?

When you finish answering these questions for the first area selected, repeat the above steps with other areas of their lives. I have given you an idea of what one phase of this plan would look like on the following page.

Our Sample Plan

Health Goals

What five things do I want my children to do when it comes to their health?

---

1. *Eat more organic whole foods*

2. *Hydrate more with living water*

3. *Exercise at least 3 times per week*

4. *Fast on Mondays and Thursdays*

5. *Eliminate dairy and most meat from their diets*

What is the first step required in order to have my children *eat more organic whole*

(Complete one sheet for each area listed above)
foods **when it comes to their health?**

Step 1 – purchase organic whole foods from health food store and watch the

"Forks Over Knives Documentary"

What resources do I already have at my disposal or what resources can I acquire easily that can assist in achieving *better health*? (books, articles, websites, exercise classes, etc…)

Living Health Program, Forks Over Knives Documentary, Home Workout

DVDs and Videos, Nutrition Guide, Workout Partners

How much time will _eat more organic foods_ **require?**

(daily/weekly/monthly)

No more than already used for shopping, preparation, and eating.

What will I establish as an accountability measure?

Develop a weekly chart containing what was cooked and eaten, use Google

Drive for updates on fat loss and weekly meeting about delicious and not so

delicious cuisine.

When crafting a plan, it is imperative that you remain flexible. Not flexible as in you are writing things in pencil because you are afraid to commit, but flexible so that there is enough wiggle room just in case there may be a small or short deviation from the original plan. If the plan is too rigid, it may seem like a burden on the family and before you share your newfound plan, I want to encourage you to work together with your spouse or other parent if they are involved in raising your child. "Teamwork makes the dream work" is a nice saying but it only works when the team works together towards the same end. Remember you are a coach not a drill sergeant but don't forget that your role as a Coach is more difficult because our children didn't sign up for the program.

They are a trust from Allah and more precious, and we have the task of finding their disciplinary threshold.

Progress and change are not one and the same; change will occur whether someone intends for it to do so or not, but progress is intentional. It becomes more and more apparent when dealing with family matters. Just think about it as it relates to marriage. Does a marriage just become better over time without effort? Of course not! It takes sincere effort on the part of both spouses to continue to have that spark in their marriage, that sweetness, that newness, and genuine appreciation. Doesn't Allah tell us how humans are ungrateful and forgetful? If we are ungrateful and forgetful when it comes to our Lord, how much easier so is the case when it comes to our spouses? Point is, parenting takes work and in order for us to improve at it, we must take consistent action towards the end we desire.

I remember hearing a quote that went something like "Champions aren't made in the ring, they are merely recognized there." This means that all of the work, the practice, the drills, the sweat, the mental fortitude, and the pain that occurred behind the scenes are what made that person into a champion not simply winning the fight in front of an audience. We may have a thankless job as parents but our reward from Allah is high and He is the All Knowing and All Seer of what we do. So we can rest assured that our benefit and reward lies with our Lord. This goes to singleness of purpose and making sure we as parents are on the same page as Coaches. If we are only concerned about our children because we want praise from others and desire to hear them say how well behaved our children are and to think we are so pious, then we are on the wrong track and should revisit our intentions.

As coaches, not only do we plan for what we want as a team but we also plan to celebrate our wins. One of the best things that winning teams do is to celebrate together! American football always makes me smile when I see the players from a winning team sneak up on a coach near the end of a game when it is apparent that they are going to win and dump Gatorade, ice and all, on the coach's head and body as a gesture of celebration. Knowing that our children crave recognition, we must create the atmosphere that when they are doing well, we see it and congratulate them on it. Funny thing is that whatever behavior we reinforce, they tend to repeat. We all want and crave that special feeling of importance and want to be reassured that we matter so one of the ways to show that is to celebrate with your children.

Make their favorite dinner, take them out to eat, buy a set of thank you cards and leave a personal note, write them a letter or poem, speak highly of them in front of others (where they can hear you), or get them something special in recognition of their growth. In today's society the people getting recognition tend to be the ones that do the most outlandish of things and have the least amount of morals. The ones that get recognition are the ones that take off their clothes and live life in the fast lane. If we as Coaches don't make it cool to do the productive things we want our children to do by feeding their craving for recognition, then our society will definitely reinforce and perpetuate its own ethics and values.

While we have addressed a few aspects of being a coach, we must also address the type of coach you are. When I was young, in my single digit years, I recall my father always wanting things in a specific manner whether it was cleaning up my room, doing my chores, or taking care of the family pets. His way of expressing things was in a direct manner and usually elevated tone, in one word, serious. As I grew older and began working with other relatives like his uncle, my great uncle, I began to notice where he may have developed some of his toughness. My great uncle was born on a farm in the southern United States and had 12 siblings. My great grandfather was a rough man who ran his farm with an iron fist and this type of behavior affected most of his children, especially the sons, in such a manner that they developed rough personalities which of course was what my father was used to and of which I became the recipient. My mother on the other hand was the oldest of six children and her mother, my grandmother, was raised in a family that was very rough and it also showed in her parenting style.

There are a few parents that are rough like the father of Umar bin Al-Khattab and we know that is not what we desire. This reminds me of my great-grand father's personality. There are parents that are so soft that they allow their children to run all over them and do whatever they please. There are those that fear their children will love them less or run away from them if they hold them accountable for anything. We must strike that balance knowing that no success comes without Allah and no success comes without work. *(The only place success comes before work is in the dictionary).*

As an example, the Prophet (عليه الصلاة و السلام) who is the best model for all times displayed his affection, love, and playfulness with all of the members in his household.

> *Anas ibn Malik (Allah be pleased with him) helped serve the Prophet (عليه الصلاة و السلام) for 10 years during his youth. He described his personal experiences with the Prophet (السلام)*

(عليه الصلاة و) *and said: "I served the Prophet*
(عليه الصلاة و السلام) *for ten years. He never said to*
me 'uff!' (a word in the Arabic language used
to express one's annoyance). And he never
said about a thing I did, 'why did you do
that?' And he never said about a thing I left,
'why did you leave that?' The Messenger of
Allah (عليه الصلاة و السلام) *was the best of people in*
character..." [Tirmidhi]

Today there are a few well known parenting styles Tracey Frost, CEO of Citibabes has described them very well.

Instinctive parenting - This might be called the "old school" method of parenting, "intuition" or simply a feeling of "go with your gut." Frost describes instinctive parenting as "very much your own personal style of parenting, usually influenced by your own upbringing." In other words, as an instinctive parent you're more likely to teach what you know and parent the way you were parented, whether you were brought up by your mother and father, siblings or another caregiver.

Attachment Parenting - In attachment parenting, the goal is for parent and child to form a strong emotional bond. The people who adopt this parenting style strive to promptly respond to their child's needs and be sensitive and emotionally available for their child at all times. The belief is that strong attachment to the parent helps the child become a more secure, empathic, peaceful human being. Fans of attachment parenting often believe in natural childbirth, a family bed, avoidance of corporal punishment, homeschooling and may be part of the anti-vaccination movement.

Helicopter parenting - "Helicopter parents constantly interact with and often interfere with their children's lives. They hover like a helicopter," explains Frost. While this kind of parenting is fairly normal to ensure the safety and security of babies and very young children, be forewarned -- smothering your child in every aspect of their life can ultimately backfire. "Too much of this style of parenting and children can become dependent on their parents' money, time and advice past their college years and into their professional careers," says Frost.

Authoritative parenting - "You live under my roof, you follow my rules!" It's a cliché, but one that parents may often find themselves speaking -- and it probably most closely mimics the authoritative parenting style. The parents who fit into this category typically establish rules and guidelines and expect their children to follow them, but the methodology is a bit more democratic than "what I say goes." For children who fail to meet the authoritative parent's expectations, the parent is more nurturing, forgiving and responsive. Their idea of discipline is to be assertive but not restrictive, to support rather than punish.

Permissive parenting - It's a child's world for permissive parents, sometimes referred to as nontraditional, indulgent parents. "They have very few demands to make of their children and rarely discipline them because they have relatively low expectations of maturity and self-control," says Frost.

If at any point the word "lenient" comes back into play, it's for this type of parent. The permissive parenting style is often evidenced by individuals who try to be more friend than parent, avoid confrontation and are generally nurturing and communicative.

Questions we must continually ask ourselves regarding our parenting style are:

- **What type of parenting style best suits my personality?**

- **How do I want my child to view my parenting?**

- **Is my parenting style flexible and compatible with my children's personality?**

- **What are 5 positive things about my parenting style?**

- **What are things that I may need to be alert for with this style?**

Now that we have spoken about discipline and feeding the need for recognition, it is absolutely imperative that we talk about becoming cheerleaders for our children. Not cheerleaders in some obnoxious way cheering on everything our child is doing, but to encourage the good behavior, laud the positive progress, and reinforce the rules that are set up. Similar to feeding the need for recognition, we encourage our children in order to teach them to continue on the right path. The lessons they may ascertain from proper encouragement are patience and perseverance, common themes throughout the entire Quran. They learn to stick on the right path no matter the challenges. They may learn the strength of the Prophets and what they had to overcome, and above all they may be more conscious of how their personal circumstances may just be a test from Allah. In this way we don't dictate how they should behave instead they are to be led by Islamic principles which you tangibly reinforce and encourage. Remember we as Coaches have a responsibility to mesh the discipline, celebration, cheerleading, and encouragement such that it provides an atmosphere of growth and development for our aspiring children.

If we want our children to grow and become better at decision-making then we must allow them to make mistakes and learn lessons from those mistakes. There has been talk in the parenting community about a parenting style that is called the 'Helicopter Parent' and that is a parent that hovers over their children and as soon as there is a challenge of problem, the parent swoops in like a rescue team and 'saves' the children. When parents exhibit this type of behavior it usually is because they love their children so much and feel the need to protect them and keep them safe. The challenge is that it creates an atmosphere of dependency while discouraging responsibility for actions. It gives children an out and unfortunately enables them to continue a type of reckless behavior because Mom or Dad or both will come to my rescue. Though I am not talking about a mistake such as selling drugs and facing jail time, I'm talking about when our children don't make the best decisions when faced with an issue or challenge. Keep in mind we must uphold justice as parents. Didn't Prophet Muhammad (عليه الصلاة و السلام) say that if Faatimah, the daughter of Muhammad, stole that he would cut her hand? He (عليه الصلاة و السلام) was the best example and justice was not only for those outside of his home, but it started within the family.

Think about it, how long would you give for your newborn child to learn to walk? Would you give her 8 months, 10 months, 12 months, or more? Or would you give her, until? Would you simply allow her as long as it took to learn to walk? She was blessed with the equipment necessary when she was born but it will take some time to strengthen those little legs. It will take more time for her to learn how to balance properly and even more time to gain the confidence needed to let go of her surrounding areas and walk all by herself. The confidence our children gain after learning to walk is evident when they snatch away from holding your hand or finger so they 'can do it on their own' and this makes all of the times they fell down, all of the times they cried. It is also evident when they made different choices – for example, when they stopped standing and chose to crawl because it was faster and simply what they were used to doing.

I remember hearing a story of a boy that was watching a chick attempt to hatch from its shell. First of all, this is a beautiful thing and an experience you can share at many museums or farms across the US. But back to the story! As the boy watched the egg roll from side to side, he saw a small hole appear and he was pretty excited and amazed at the process. He noticed the hole get a little larger and grew impatient because the process seemed to be taking so long in his mind. Well after a few minutes, he decided to help the chick by making the hole larger and the chick would be able to get out of the shell quicker. Well, the chick did get out faster and it was due to the boy making the hole larger and cracking the shell. Unfortunately what the boy didn't know *(and I didn't know either!)* was that the challenge that was before the chick, using his beak to break the shell, was put there by Allah to strengthen the beak so that the chick could eat and survive after leaving the shell and starting a new life. Well, since the chick lost the ability to strengthen its beak by hardening it, it couldn't eat properly and later died. His ***helping*** was really ***hurting*** the chick.

Don't be the boy wanting to help a chick when in reality we are hurting it due to our impatience. Remember this when you as the Mother or Father want to help your little one emerge from their shell, it may be that this shell is there to make them stronger in order to succeed at what life has planned for them. Use your good judgment, yes, but allow your children the space and time they need to strengthen their skills and character so they can be prepared to live a vigorous life. There must be a time after the lessons are taught, after practice has been done, that we allow our children to enter the ring. After all it is only after they enter the ring that they may emerge victorious and be recognized as champions!

Your C 3 Assessment

So, here is your third homework assignment! In order to assess and, in shaa Allah, become more effective with C 3— the Coaching role – take some time now to answer the following questions in a personal journal or via the online document:

1. How can I become more effective in my role as Coach?

2. What do I need to do in order to be better at discipline?

3. How can I be better at recognizing and cheerleading my child's successes?

4. What ways can we celebrate our wins together that is fun for all?

5. How would I describe my coaching style?

6. How can I be sure not to impede my children's growth by swooping in to save them?

Access your C 3 worksheet at:

OutstandingMuslimParents.com/c3

Chapter 7   Being Conscious of the Three

C's in Our Daily Lives

Some experts state that it takes 21 days to establish a new habit. Alhamdulillah, we have something that can assist us in a much quicker fashion and help us stay on task. We know that Islam is replete with people that have accepted Islam and completely changed their lives seemingly in moments. We have examples of famous companions like Umar bin Al-Khattab who went from an extreme of wanting to kill the Messenger of Allah (عليه الصلاة و السلام) to submitting to Allah and becoming a follower of Islam all in the same day! We know of women that were not religious and were very promiscuous in their lives that went on to accept Islam, practice hijab and adopt piety and hayaa (shyness). These changes may have taken time or been immediate.

I'm a strong believer that change happens in a moment. The moment when we decide that things will change and have the resolve to follow through. See it is those people that accepted Islam and were firm it in so much so that when the ayah was revealed with the explicit prohibition of alcohol, it was said that alcohol was flowing in the streets of Madinah. Change happened in a moment.

We have the power of du'a and we have the opportunity to offer du'a at any time and pretty much anywhere. It is very simple to offer du'a after we pray and ask Allah for what we desire including being an outstanding parent and everything that comes with that. We pray and say al-Fatihah at least 17 times per day if we only pray the obligatory prayers -- we say it in each and every rak'at. Just as the repetition helps us with being more conscious of Allah and His Majesty, we should

56

use this lesson in repetition to be more precise and intentional in our du'a so that we can develop the new habits, skills, and emotional fortitude that we all need as parents raising righteous children.

How can we be more conscious of the Three C's in our

daily life?

There are numerous ways and I'm going to ask you to be clear when talking to yourself. Yes, I said talking to yourself. We all do it; as a matter of fact, we are in dialogue with ourselves more than anyone else could be. We ask ourselves questions, get clarification, praise ourselves when something goes well, say things to ourselves that we would not dare let someone else say, and we do it day in and day out. So when you are talking to yourself and dealing with your children, I want to ask you to train your brain to ask, **"What role am I in right now?"**

For example, let's say you have a 5 year old son:

The adhan goes off for salatul 'Asr and that means it's time for salah. Both you and your child hear the adhan. **Ask yourself, "What role am I in right now?"**

You know that your 5 year old isn't obligated to pray but you want to do everything in your power to help your child like praying and you want them to desire to pray. Now if you have a pattern that is working and your child pays attention during salah, knows how to perform wudu, how to offer salah properly, and is well behaved, alhamdulillah, you surely are raising a unique child and Allah has made it easier for you. However, if you have more than one child and they don't all

act like the above or your child isn't up to par, then there are some things you can work on.

Understanding that we all want to be recognized and feel accepted, ask yourself, "What can I do to help my 5 year old feel accepted **and recognized?"** Be sure to listen to the answer.

You might teach your child how to perform wudu, have them set the prayer rug up properly, have them call the iqamah for boys, or have them do a double check to make sure the hair is properly covered for girls. You may also remind them of the importance of salah and when they perform it properly, congratulate them once it's over and tell them how proud you are of them. You can also do an after salah recharge meaning you don't just break after the salah; you hug each other and express how you love each other.

This is one of the highlights in my home. Everyone hugs and tells the other person that they love them. How often do we hear how people are still hurting in adulthood because they were not raised in an encouraging home? Let us nurture each other, let our family know how important they are no matter the size, and allow us to attach that extra love and caring to a special and peaceful time after we pray to The Sublime.

So, what role(s) were you performing in the above salah scenario? *Were you a Celebrity? Were you a Confidant? Were you a Coach?* In the above scenario with salah, you are playing two roles, mainly the Celebrity and the Coach. As the Celebrity, you are modeling the proper behavior when it comes to salah because you perform wudu and get prepared to pray. You are also the Coach because you are training your children how to perform wudu and helping them be a part of the process and team even if the team consists of only you two.

Let's take another example and this time let's say you have a daughter of 5 years old.
She may be in the process of developing a liking for a certain clothing style. Of my daughters, 5 years old tended to be the age when they started playing dress up and discovered the power of dressing themselves and looking in the mirror after every wardrobe change. Now say that our little fashionista puts on her mother's scarf and is imitating her mother during her wardrobe change. Ask yourself, **"What role am I in right now?"**

You may consider praising how beautiful that headscarf makes her outfit look, how righteous she looks, and how she would look so beautiful in her own scarf and you have to go shopping in order to find some for her.

59

You may also consider showing her how beautiful the khimar can be by having a fashion show and having her play a part. You may show your daughter how versatile the khimar is in different cultures and areas of the world and its splendor.

You may show her how respectable our culture is by contrasting with such things as the Marilyn Monroe statue that is in Chicago, Illinois. There is a larger than life statue that has

Marilyn Monroe who was not known for her chastity in a famous pose where her skirt was blown upwards exposing her underwear right in the middle of the city. Alhamdulillah our children have a

natural shyness and would likely feel uncomfortable

if their undergarments or their mother's

undergarments were showing like this statue's.

Of course, our children's understanding and vocabulary may be limited so keep in mind that images help tell a story and may assist in communicating things that may be challenging to articulate.

What role(s) were you performing in the above hijab/clothing scenario? *Were you a Celebrity? Were you a Confidant? Were you a Coach?* In the above scenario, you were playing all three of the roles! You assumed the role of:
- The Confidant by exposing the fight against modesty and how Islam honors our women.

- The Celebrity by modeling or positively recognizing the behavior you desire.

The Coach by cheerleading and encouraging Islamic behavior in dress and in teaching how the dress is properly worn. You can help them understand that new trend of tight abayahs doesn't fit the category of being covered since seeing the shape of the person negates hijab...and Allah knows best.

When we are conscious of the things going around us, we keep our minds sharp and become better at recognizing our roles and the better we recognize our roles, the better we can be at executing them and have fun while doing so. I have to admit; sometimes it can be boring and frustrating to do something over and over aimlessly. Think of something many people take as fun or exhilarating like riding on a roller coaster but follow the description of riding the roller coaster with "over and over aimlessly" and notice how that exhilarating experience just seems boring now? We must be cognizant of the feelings we associate with our seemingly menial tasks and understand that we can shape our child's view based on how we interpret things. Our children can see offering salah as something done over and over aimlessly or they can see it as a special time to communicate with the Creator of everything. The difference is our perspective.

The great part is that we can change our entire perspective by changing our vocabulary a few words at a time from words that do not help us to words that empower us. For example, when you feel overwhelmed you may use the word **frustrated** or **frustration**, I challenge you to stop saying you are frustrated and say that you are *fascinated.* See, as a parent we are already masters at reframing things for our children and we should also be able to use some of that good medicine for ourselves. Another quick example of gratefulness, have you ever said you had a bad day? If so, change that saying because you can appear ungrateful for a day that Allah gave you to get closer to Him and we know that Prophet Muhammad (عليه الصلاة و السلام) said,

> *"How amazing is the affair of the believer. There is good for him in everything and that is for not one but the believer. If good times come his way, he expresses gratitude to Allah and that is good for him, and if hardship comes his way, he endures it patiently and that is better for him."* [Muslim]

It is much easier to describe what we used to call a bad day as a *character building day* because the trial or fitnah that you have come across may be an opportunity for you to build your character and Allah knows best. We let our children know to look at things from a different perspective and I tell you that if we took our own advice in this area more, we would be more fulfilled, Alhamdulillah.

BEING CONSCIOIUS OF THE THREE C'S IN OUR DAILY LIVES

Chapter 8   The Three E's of Parenting

In parenting, many times our focus is misplaced and we measure our effectiveness in ways that may be counterproductive. What I mean by this is many parents look at their children's behavior as sort of a measurement stick when that may not necessarily be the best gauge. Parenting is about you as a parent, how you feel, act, influence, love, and care for your child.

Though there are many great characteristics outstanding parents exhibit, I think that if we focus on three in particular we will be able to encompass many of the rest.

E 1 -- ENGAGING

Engage with Communication - To engage is to make an effort by taking the necessary steps to build connection with your child. Engaging takes many forms and the quickest route to engagement is simply speaking with your child. Please note that 'speaking with' is different than 'speaking to' your child. When you speak _with_ what you are doing is also offering a listening ear to hear what your child has to say and how they feel. When you speak to, you are telling, commanding, delegating, and are not looking for any feedback or response. Let's make it a point to speak more _with_ our children.

Communicating with your children tends to show them that you care even if they are hesitant to express that emotion. Remember the power of asking questions, once you ask a question your brain focuses on finding an answer for what was asked before proceeding to something else or that awkward feeling creeps in.

When speaking with your child asking simple questions like "what is your favorite part about Islam?" or "what do you like the most about Ramadan?" and listening for the response shows them they have a voice, validates that voice, and indicates your desire to learn more about them and their likes. You may ask your daughters about the concept of hijab and how they feel about it. Now keep in mind that you are their parent and they may feel the desire to say what you want them to say instead of how they truly feel but you are the Confidant and can decipher when someone is trying to dupe you, right? In that case, reassure them that it is okay to have a range of feelings about this and that you know of others that may have felt the same way. Then you go into your Confidant mode by educating and helping your child explore their full range of ideas and feelings. Keep in mind that a situation like the difficult conversation I just mentioned may not be a one shot conversation, this may take a few weeks or even months but keep the door open for discussion and continue to engage by discussing other topics that you know they enjoy.

Engage with Physical Affection -- We have the absolute best example in everything and there are so many examples of our beloved Prophet (عليه الصلاة و السلام) in his dealing with children that we can emulate with no problem.

> *Anas ibn Malik (may Allah be pleased with him), reported: I never saw anyone who was more compassionate towards children than Allah's Messenger (عليه الصلاة و السلام). His son Ibrahim was in the care of a wet nurse in the hills around Madinah. He would go there, and we would go with him, and*

he would enter the house, pick up his son and kiss him, then come back. [Muslim]

Touching and being touched in ways that help us to feel appreciated and cared for is an essential ingredient to an optimal health care program. Parents soothe and nurture children by stroking, cuddling, rocking, and hugging them. Children invite such contact as part of their daily diet, both to meet their basic acceptance needs and for comfort when they are frightened or unsettled.

> *It was narrated that 'Aisha (may Allah be pleased with her) said: A Bedouin came to the Prophet (عليه الصلاة و السلام) and said: Do you kiss children? We do not kiss them. The Prophet (عليه الصلاة و السلام) said: "What can I do for you if Allah has removed mercy from your heart?"*
> *[Bukhari]*

The same is true for adults. Gentle, soothing touch, at an appropriate time, from an appropriate trusted person can be a very effective antidote to the bodily tension induced by daily interpersonal conflicts, noise assault, and other challenges associated with life on earth.

> *Narrated Abu Hurairah: The Messenger of Allah (عليه الصلاة و السلام) kissed Al-Hasan bin Ali while Al-Aqra' bin Habis At-Tamim was sitting beside him. Al-Aqra said, "I have ten children and I have never kissed anyone of them," The Messenger of Allah (الصلاة و السلام عليه) cast a look at him and said, "Whoever is not merciful to others will not be treated mercifully." [Bukhari]*

Dr. Rene Spitz first published his findings in 1945 that established that **gentle touch** is necessary for the good health of babies. Babies, who were raised in orphanages where staff sizes were so small that they were not held and cuddled, suffered adverse health effects. Some babies literally "withered away" and died. Numerous subsequent studies confirmed these findings. Studies found that babies born prematurely who were kept in incubators but not touched or stroked failed to thrive. Today it is common practice for both hospital staff and parents to set aside an ample amount of time for touching, tickling, and stroking premature babies. This practice results in healthier babies, bi'ithnillah.

In a hadith narrated by Usama bin Zaid:

> *Allah's Messenger* (عليه الصلاة و السلام) *used to put me on (one of) his thighs and put Al-Hasan ibn 'Ali on his other thigh, and then embrace us and say, "O Allah! Please be merciful to them, as I am merciful to them." [Bukhari]*

Prophet Muhammad (عليه الصلاة و السلام) never held back his love for the children and always expressed his fondness to them. In one hadith Abu Hurairah (may Allah be pleased with him) narrated:

> *I went along with Allah's Messenger* (السلام و عليه الصلاة) *at a time during the day but he did not talk to me and I did not talk to him until he reached the market of Banu Qainuqa`. He came back to the tent of Fatimah and said, "Is the little chap (meaning Al-Hasan) there?" We were under the impression that his mother had detained him in order to bathe him and dress him and garland him with sweet garland. Not much time had passed that he*

(Al-Hasan) came running until both of them embraced each other, thereupon Allah's Messenger (peace and blessings be upon him) said, "O Allah, I love him; love him and love one who loves him." [Muslim]

This may be one of the easiest areas for us as parents because most of us are able to easily hug and kiss our children. For those of us who due to our personalities or life experiences have difficulty showing physical affection, consider the benefits and take it one step at a time. Start with a pat on the head, a playful hug or kiss and before you know it Allah may help you break down your resistance. Just remember, that as your children get older, they may be embarrassed by the affection -- but it doesn't matter if they don't understand the dynamics and positive energy that is exchanged. What matters is that you still engage them and show them love just as you did when they were young.

Your E 1 Reflections

Take some time now to go to the OMP website to view the video and complete the accompanying worksheet to reflect on your own engagement practices with your children. To view the bonus video lesson that corresponds with this section, visit the following link: *OutstandingMuslimParents.com/engage*

E 2 -- EQUIPPING

As we continue engaging and building the relationship we desire or as we work at creating a breakthrough, we must equip our children to navigate life. Equipping can be seen as giving our children what they need in order to make correct decision when they address life's issues so that as they live life and encounter new things they do so with sure footing and are less apt to be caught off guard.

When we consider Islam, we can say that we as Muslims have been equipped with everything we need to win. We have been given instructions on the purpose of life, how to worship, and how to get to paradise. We have been given all of this through the best example in our Prophet (الصلاة و السلام عليه) who was guided by the Creator, the All Knowing. We have been given examples of those people who were successful as well as stories of previous societies that were destroyed in order that we might learn from their errors. Allah, ta'ala, has equipped us with what it takes to win and what it takes to lose and the decisions are now up to us. May Allah make us successful in our quest for paradise and forgive us our sins and shortcomings and allow us to be parents that raise up strong Muslims that will be a shield for us on the final day, Ameen.

There are many things that our society is filled with that contradict Islam and our way of life as Muslims. As parents it is our responsibility to properly analyze what is going on in society and know how Islam would address it. Issues that many times affect our own Muslim communities include:

- Homosexuality
- Racism
- Bullying
- Classism/Sexism
- Alcohol/drugs
- Violence/Murder
- Immodesty/Zina
- Dishonesty/Vice

As Muslims, we know that Islam addresses all of these issues and does so in a comprehensive fashion. Islam also requires us to find the answers while parenting requires us to convey these lessons to our children via Islamic solutions that they can understand. A clear message to us from our Lord is where Allah, ta'ala, tells us:

يَٰٓأَيُّهَا ٱلَّذِينَ ءَامَنُوا۟ قُوٓا۟ أَنفُسَكُمْ وَأَهْلِيكُمْ نَارًا وَقُودُهَا ٱلنَّاسُ وَٱلْحِجَارَةُ عَلَيْهَا مَلَٰٓئِكَةٌ غِلَاظٌ شِدَادٌ لَّا يَعْصُونَ ٱللَّهَ مَآ أَمَرَهُمْ وَيَفْعَلُونَ مَا يُؤْمَرُونَ ﴿٦﴾

"O you who believe! Save yourselves and your families against a Fire (Hell) whose fuel is men and stones, over which are (appointed) angels stern (and) severe, who disobey not, (from executing) the Commands they receive from Allah, but do that which they are commanded" [al-Tahreem 66:6]

Equipping our children is not unlike preparing for a trip. There are essentials that are needed for a trip and there are extras to be prepared for just in case something doesn't go as planned. There are things that we want to accomplish during the trip and we prepare as best we can in advance by making sure we are properly prepared. Some things we may purchase prior to going and other things we may wait until we arrive at the destination to buy. As parents, we must provide the overall guidance for our children by sharing with them principles that help them towards success.

In order to properly equip our children, we must be familiar with the terrain and the obstacles that our children may encounter. Though the landscape is different depending on wherever you are in the world, one thing is for certain, Islamic principles don't budge. Understanding that we cannot change Islam to our circumstances, we must equip ourselves so that we can properly apply the Islamic principles to our circumstances.

You may be asking, "Okay, how do I do that?" Well, first of all, we must become closer to Allah by doing what we can to better understand the Qur'an. If we expect our children to come closer to the Book of Allah, then we must practice what we preach. Remember that we don't ever want to give our children the typical hypocritical advice of "do what I say do, don't do what I do!"

E 2 Reflections

At this juncture, I want you to take a moment to reflect on

what your true  relationship is with

the Book of Allah. In His Book, Allah

teaches us so much through

stories. In the lives of the Prophets, there are stories of

triumph, sadness, and family drama. We can learn the

importance of trusting in Allah, having patience, family vs.

relatives, sibling rivalry, marriage, polygyny, disobedience, true failure, heartbreak, and much more. It is up to us to gather the lessons, understand them, and be able to relate them to our children in a way in which they can understand in shaa Allah. There is no better equipping than comes from the Creator of all that exists of the seen and unseen and for that we are grateful.

To view a bonus video lesson that corresponds with this section, visit the following link:

OutstandingMuslimParents.com/equip

E-3 EMPOWERING

Okay, we have engaged and gotten through to our children while communicating with them regularly. We are equipping them with the proper tools for success and do what we can for them to understand the Quran's magnificence and relevance for all times with the lessons that Allah has provided.

Now, we must allow them the opportunity to be tested. I know, we are parents and many times we want to protect our child from things that happen because we don't know how they'll respond, however one way you can test your child is to let them have the independence they so desire (and appropriate for their age and maturation) and make choices for themselves when you are not around. Don't worry, it's not the end of the world and your job as a parent is not over.

For example, let's say you have children that love sweets like my children do and you have already discussed the importance of patience or telling the truth or asking before taking action. Then you leave the cookies, cake, or sweets out and allow them to make a decision. They may decide to ask first, wait patiently till later, or take and eat some. Both give us something to work with. Let's not lose the ability to teach by failing to quiz. Like my mother taught me, when you cheat, you only cheat yourself.

Quizzing our children verbally or through lessons we put together for them or physically by allowing them to make decisions while we observe helps us better our parenting techniques. Now keep in mind, the above test with cookies was for a small child, but it doesn't matter the age of your child -- what matters is that you prepare the quiz. How effective and accurate do you think a teacher would be if they constantly taught your child in class but never quizzed or tested them? Your testing can consist of questioning like asking what your child's opinion is on dating, bullying, or classism within Muslim schools. Yes, I know we would rather not speak of such things in our Muslim schools, but dating, drug and alcohol use, sex, bullying, racism, and classism are just some of the sicknesses that society has wreaked on our community as a whole. So ask your children where they stand or better yet, ask them what they would do or suggest in order to tackle the issue and why they would make that suggestion.

Here's a little tip for the parents whose children may say "I don't know" too often when asked pointed questions; after they say "I don't know", I want you to respond, "okay, I know you don't know, but if you did know.....", then repeat the question. This allows our child to not be stumped and settle for an 'I don't know' type of shutdown.

Let me repeat these simple steps to empowering our children. We get through to them with *engagement*; we then properly *equip* them with Islam and its applicability in life; and finally, we *empower* them by allowing them the opportunity to make decisions and learn lessons firsthand.

E 3 Reflections

Empowerment is one of the greatest things we can do for our children and has been shown to be one of the prominent characteristics in youth and young adults who exhibit high self-confidence, willingness to accept challenges, and excel at leadership. Reflect on how well your parenting may be empowering your children by viewing the bonus video at the following link: OutstandingMuslimParents.com/empower

THE THREE E'S OF PARENTING

Chapter 9   Where My Focus as a Parent

Should Be

Knowing where your focus as a parent should be is essential to living without unnecessary stress. As parents, we have enough things to stress us out and adding more stress from inside the home can be debilitating and cause you to feel that you have to find a way to escape the household even if it just be for a few days or maybe even a few hours!

We wear many hats -- cook, cleaner, teacher, nurse, counselor, cheerleader, consoler, nutritionist, and many more. With that being said, it is far too easy to lose ourselves in our role as parent and to neglect ourselves. This isn't good for anyone, especially us. We must be sure to take care of the other areas of our lives in order to have a semblance of balance.

I often teach on the very important topic of balance and find it hard to single out a group of people that need to find balance more than parents. Though we likely won't stop juggling so many hats and responsibilities, there is a way to nurture yourself and make sure you are taking care of *you*. See, if you are not taking care of yourself, then you won't be up to par for anyone else and then everyone suffers. As a husband and father, there are many demands that are put on me by my family and by Allah ta'ala --responsibilities I must fulfill to the best of my ability. I have learned to accept the fact that life is not static and most things are out of our control, but if I can get anywhere close to balance, I will be happy.

Let me share a formula that has helped me greatly and, in shaa Allah, will help you in caring for yourself. First, there is a well known philosophy in the West that basically means 'take care of me and I'll take care of you'. I have heard the saying several different ways but the meaning is the same such as *'one hand washes the other'* or *'scratch my back and I'll scratch yours'.* Well, as a parent we don't have this type of thinking when it comes to our children. We don't bathe them, love them, and feed them for them to only do something for us in return. As a matter of fact, that type of philosophy is hardly from our deen. Think about it, aren't we told to do things for the sake of Allah and we will be rewarded? Think about hijrah and if it is done for the sake of marriage or any other reason except purely for the sake of Allah, then the reward is with the marriage or the people but not Allah ta'ala.

> *On the authority of Abu Hafs, Umar Ibn al-Khattab, who said: 'I heard the Messenger of Allah:*
>
> *"The actions are innama (only, certainty) tied to the intentions and every person will earn that which he intended. Therefore, he whose migration was for Allah and His Messenger* (عليه الصلاة و السلام) *then his migration will be for Allah and His Messenger; and he whose migration was to achieve some worldly gain or to take a woman in marriage, then his migration will be for that for which he migrated." [Bukhari and Muslim]*

Consider this simple philosophy that is summed up in this little phrase, "I will take care of me for you, if you will take care of you for me." If we focus on being better, learning our deen, and practicing our way of life then we become better for all of those with whom we come into contact.

In our lives and quest for balance, we must realize that we have different areas of our life and we should be aware of them so as to give each area its proper time. The following are a few areas that I think most people can relate to and I believe lead to a healthy balance, so I'll call these areas the Six Areas to Healthy Balance. *(Yours may be slightly different)*

Spiritual Health	How you study, practice, and teach Islam?
Physical Health	What you do for optimum energy, fitness, and vitality?
Family Health	What you are doing with your family that generates love?
Emotional Health	How your emotional needs are being met?
Financial Health	What plans you are working on for financial success?
Career Health	What do you do outside the home that is fulfilling?

Six Areas to Healthy Balance

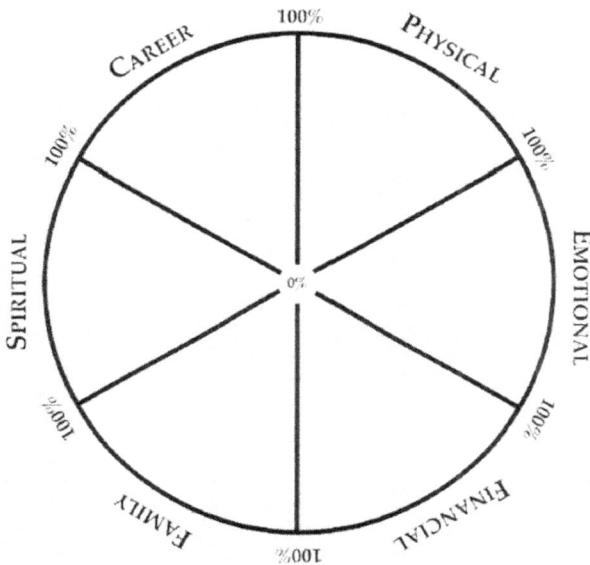

The above diagram depicts the 6 aspects of healthy balance that I just described. What you are supposed to do with the above diagram is fill in the triangles to whatever level you feel that you are at percentage-wise. If you feel that you are at 50% in your financial health area, then shade it in from the center to the halfway mark. Then proceed to every other area that applies and do the same. After completing the exercise,

ask yourself some of the questions below and provide
answers to each applicable section.

**Am I satisfied with being at ____% in the Spiritual area
of my life?   Yes/No**

Why or Why not?

_____

_____

_____

_____

**Am I satisfied with being at ____% in the Physical area of
my life?   Yes/No**

Why or Why not?

_____

_____

_____

_____

Am I satisfied with being at ____% in the Family area of my life?   Yes/No

Why or Why not?

_____

_____

_____

_____

Am I satisfied with being at ____% in the Emotional area of my life?   Yes/No

Why or Why not?

_____

_____

_____

_____

Am I satisfied with being at ____% in the Financial area of my life?   Yes/No

Why or Why not?

_____

_____

_____

_____

Am I satisfied with being at ____% in the Career area of my life?   Yes/No

Why or Why not?

_____

_____

_____

Then ask yourself:

What 3 things can I do within the next 7 days to begin improving my Spiritual health?

_____

_____

_____

_____

What 3 things can I do within the next 7 days to begin improving my Physical health?

_____

_____

_____

_____

What 3 things can I do within the next 7 days to begin improving my Family health?

_____

_____

_____

_____

What 3 things can I do within the next 7 days to begin improving my Emotional health?

_____

_____

_____

_____

What 3 things can I do within the next 7 days to begin improving my Financial health?

_____

_____

_____

_____

What 3 things can I do within the next 7 days to begin improving my Career health?

_____

_____

_____

_____

Next, ask yourself:

What resources or knowledge do I already have that can assist me with my Spiritual health?

_____

_____

What resources or knowledge do I already have that can assist me with my Physical health?

_____

_____

What resources or knowledge do I already have that can assist me with my Family health?

_____

_____

What resources or knowledge do I already have that can assist me with my Emotional health?

_____

_____

What resources or knowledge do I already have that can assist me with my Financial health?

_____

_____

What resources or knowledge do I already have that can assist me with my Career health?

_____

_____

Write out the reasons why you choose to improve in each area of your life's health and be specific.

I have trained thousands of people on these exercises alone and can't stress how significant an impact the clarity in each area of life provides. I encourage you to run in the opposite direction of mediocrity and complete the exercises above in detail. The reward is absolutely worth it!

As you work on yourself continually, you will see improvement and progress, in shaa Allah. Start with seeking the pleasure of Allah in each area and with your efforts and become an outstanding human in the process which, with the help of Allah, will make you an outstanding parent.

We know that self-assessment tools help us to better analyze ourselves and assist in helping us develop the best personal solutions. For more self assessment tools, please see the Outstanding Muslim Parents Academy at OutstandingMuslimParents.com/academy. We hope this is one of the first steps that you are taking on the lifelong journey of personal and family development, in shaa Allah.

WHERE MY FOCUS AS A PARENT SHOULD BE

Chapter 10   Closing Thoughts

As you know there is no cookie cutter when it comes to parenting; there are just solid Islamic principles that guide us and different strategies that can be adjusted to our needs at specific times. Perhaps that is why we should be selfish when it comes to parenting. You may be wondering about selfishness and thinking that we shouldn't exhibit that type of behavior, but before you start to frown up as you read this, let me explain. Allah tells us to compete with each other in good deeds. If there's one characteristic that we can see in our very small children is that they are inherently all about themselves. They are plain selfish and alhamdulillah, they must be in order to preserve themselves and secretly we enjoy it.

I want you to be selfish when it comes to encompassing good deeds and the pleasure of Allah ta'ala. If you have daughters, you have a special opportunity that has not been connected to sons. Remember that our Prophet (عليه الصلاة و السلام) is reported to have said,

> *Narrated By 'Aisha: A lady along with her two daughters came to me asking me (for some alms), but she found nothing with me except one date which I gave to her and she divided it between her two daughters, and then she got up and went away. Then the Prophet came in and I informed him about this story. He* (السلام*
>
> *و* (عليه الصلاة و) *said, "Whoever is in charge of (put to test by) these daughters and treats them generously, then they will act as a shield for him from the (Hell) Fire." [Bukhari]*

Narrated by Abu Sa'id al-Khudri: The Prophet (عليه الصلاة و السلام) said: If anyone cares for three daughters, disciplines them, marries them, and does good to them, he will go to Paradise. [Abu Dawood]

Hadhrat Anas (radiyallahu anhu) reports Rasulullah (عليه الصلاة و السلام) said, "The person who successfully brings up two daughters until they reach maturity, then on the day of Qiyamah (Judgment) I and that person will be like this (Rasulullah indicated closeness by bringing together his index and middle fingers). [Muslim]

Imam Bukhari has brought several ahadith in his book Adab ul Mufrad, stating that the person, who has two or three daughters, and he gives them an Islamic upbringing then those very daughters will become a shield for him from the fire of Jahannam (Hell).

The person who brings up three daughters, gets them married, and thereafter maintains affable relationship with them; will enter Jannah (paradise).   [Abu Dawood]

I wanted (and was blessed) to bring up daughters first because in Western society just as in the Arab society of Quraysh, it was more pleasing to people to have sons than daughters. We may not bury our daughters alive and but in this society there is much more excitement when someone is said to be pregnant with a son or has sons than daughters. The parallels are plenty and these are the times our children are growing up in.

We have the opportunity as parents to acquire lots of barakah (blessings) as we work to engage, equip, and empower our children. Let's not forget the wonderful hadith that should leave every parent full of hope:

The Prophet (عليه الصلاة و السلام) said: "When a man (Muslim man or woman) dies, his good deeds come to an end except three: ongoing charity, beneficial knowledge and righteous offspring who will pray for him." [Muslim]

All of the stress, worry, heartache, crying, and headaches are worth it when we take responsibility for raising our child to be righteous. If we can do such a thing (which isn't easy) and succeed, then it is absolutely worth it. Can you imagine coming before Allah and wondering where all of these deeds that are on the good side of your scale came from and you learn that they are from the prayers of your righteous children? SubhanAllah, let's do what we can with what we have and understand that through it all the end result is worth it.

As I complete the writing of this book, I would like to share a personal experience. My family recently suffered from the loss of a dear relative. My father-in-law passed away and it hit my family pretty hard. It is amazing that we cherish things more when they are gone and that we recognize the finality of life sometimes only in the face of death. My father-in-law wasn't Muslim although he received da'wah -- Allah didn't choose him to partake in this beautiful blessing of Islam. Looking at these dynamics it leads us right back to the Qur'an where Allah shares the story of Ibrahim who was an ummah to himself whose father rejected the call. It also shows us that no matter whom we wish, it is Allah that makes Muslims and reminds us of the Year of Grief when our Prophet (عليه الصلاة و السلام) was very sad because our mother Ummul Mu'mineen (Mother of the Believers) Khadijah bin Khuwaylid passed and Abu Talib, the uncle of Rasulullah (عليه الصلاة و السلام), who protected him against his enemies, died and refused to accept Islam even on his deathbed.

We are grateful to be Muslims and happy that our eyes were opened to the right path. It is amazing to know that we have the opportunity to change the world for the better by investing in our children by helping them craft their Muslim identities so that they can be the problem solvers in such a trying time. Let's be sure to hug often and love our children hard in recognition of the trust Allah has put under our care and equip them to grow through spiritual, family and social challenges in this life as they continue their journey along with us to our ultimate end which we pray is paradise-- where we shall all return to Allah, ameen!

<u>Parenting Resources</u>

Muslim Parenting Association
MuslimParentingAssociation.org
An association dedicated to providing valuable resources and best practices to parents intending to excel at raising Muslim children.

Outstanding Muslim Parents, Inc.
OutstandingMuslimParents.com
An online and offline company focused on providing parents with the training, coaching, and tools they need to raise an outstanding family.

Programs Include: OMP Online Academy, Setting Standards 6 CD Course, Online Webinars, Offline Workshops, Keynote Speaking, Outstanding Parents Television Episodes, and Exciting parents and youth retreats.

OutstandingMuslimParents.tv

About the Author

Nazir Al-Mujaahid was born in the Midwestern United States to a Christian family and attended Christian private schools up to high school. He went on a soul search and disowned all 'organized religion' but kept the belief in One God. His studies lead all over the place but he ended up being convinced that Islam is the unadulterated truth and became a Muslim in 1994.

After many trials with his relatives regarding his new way of life, he chose to embark on a new path which broke off most of the habits from his past including how to raise children. Getting married at a young age and beginning a family, he made it a point to change the thinking, traditions, and style in which he was raised in order to break away from the generational non-Muslim think his relatives were accustomed to.

He became an entrepreneur and experienced success in several industries including network marketing and internet marketing. He learned leadership, teambuilding, and system creation and began a lifelong learning journey to include human behavior, neuroscience, neuro linguistic programming, child psychology and more.

He focused on serving the underserved Muslim community in one of his first online ventures at MuslimMoneyMan.com and then after seeing the collapse of several Muslim families specifically dealing with their children, he was encouraged to share the systems he and his family created in order to strengthen the family unit and stop the loss of our children.

He founded the OMP Online Academy in 2012 and continues to speak and train parents worldwide including creating and

About the Author

hosting a television show on Huda aptly named Outstanding Parents. His mission is to empower the ummah by establishing strong Muslim families by equipping parents and empowering the youth!

For more info; please visit **OutstandingMuslimParents.com**